HELLO
I'M A...

MILLENNIAL

The New Face of Modern Management and Training

By Monique L. Rodgers

1

Dedication

This book is dedicated to God who is truly my everything. To my best friend and sister Tamara Huff for always believing in me and pushing me to greatness. To my mom Genise Rodgers To my godmother Mama T for her daily encouragement and texts. To my wonderful siblings Abbigail, Daniel, Emily, Melissa, and Shanell. To my best friend in Heaven Tahshal Fletcher Kimani for always believing in me and being my angel. To Joshua Porter for always being there to laugh when I needed someone. To my best friend Tiffany Sumo for being the wind beneath my wings and helping me to always remember to aim higher in life. To Charles Hammond thank you for always praying for me and encouraging me. To Ramond Walker thank you for always encouraging me to do more. To Trecie Williams for never giving up on me. To all of my professors from Oral Roberts University and Colorado Technical University. I am so thankful for each of you and to every young aspiring manager that has ever dreamed of being a manager I celebrate you. May this book be an inspiration that helps you become all that you need to be in life and more.

Table of Contents

Who You Calling a Millennial?

I remember as a young teenager growing up in school before everyone went to their lockers there was always someone in the hall to monitor students that were being disruptive. The hall monitors would help to break up disputes and fights at school. There would be students yelling at one another in disarray and anger some would yell the words, who are you calling a loser? There was something powerful about the words *who are you calling a so and so* that rang in my ear. It was defiance versus inferiority of I may appear to be this but this is who I really am. The same is so for millennial leaders. They may appear to be a youngster that is unskilled and wet behind the ears so to speak but in all actuality they are the leading pioneers of business and management. Management today has helped to uncover a new defining face of leadership that has gained precedence in businesses all over the world.

Millennial leaders are now the new iconic symbol in terms of business leadership in companies all over the world. Perhaps you have seen them before they are eclectic, energized, and tech savvy. They are the new generation of managers known as the "*Millennials*". Millennials are defined as being born between the 1980's-2000. This type of leader has been named as a millennial leader in management. Millennial leaders are the new uprising of leaders in management today. From all over the world young adult leaders have taken a new approach to leadership and are now the new faces of managers, trainers, and global leaders. According to Pollak, "In a recent study from Pew Research the study revealed that only forty percent of millennials even acknowledged with the word "millennial," while nearly eighty percent of those aged fifty-one to sixty nine consider themselves part of the Baby Boomer age group. Leadership that is entrusted into someone that is a millennial is becoming more popular than it has been in prior years. There are a lot of factors to consider about Millennials: They are the largest U.S. generational peer group ever, with roughly eighty million members. Within most places of employment, millennials have to fight even harder to secure a job in management than most because of the lack of candor that most employers feel that they do not have. Employers feel that millennials are careless and often arrive late for work, and that they prefer texting over conversation, and they are always calling in to work to request off from work. (Pollak, 2015) Millennials manage much more collaboratively than any other generation," according to Brad Karsh, founder and CEO of JB Training Solutions and author of *Manager 3.0: A Millennial's Guide to Rewriting the Rules of Management*. Part of their influence is derived from the generation that they were born in. They grew up doing more activities in groups than previous generations, Karsh says, "more clubs, more games, more camps, more things where they work together. (McCleary, 2016) That translates to leaders who look for lots of input. "Less command-and-control, more team-based, says Jim Moffatt, managing director of Deloitte Global. The millennial has the proven talent and the ability to provide mastery in their management skills. In my research on millennial leaders I have discovered that millennial leaders can provide improved management to companies and also offer the best to employers through creating innovative solutions that are most efficient to the organizations. Millennials bring an energy and excitement to the workplace. Millennial leaders aspire to lead effectively. The training programs in the past years have not been effective for the future of management that is to come. Millennial leadership is more prominent now than it was years ago. Leaders today that were born between 1980-2000 are rising to the challenge of leadership and stepping out as aspiring leaders to train other leaders to become successful in leadership as managers. Leaders that were once turned away due to lack of experience and expertise are now gravitating to management positions. According to Enrique, the trends that capture workplace training and development are changing in so many ways the *knowledge economy* is growing and becoming an inevitable part of the modern business structure.

Jobs are becoming more fluid and specialized. The aging of the workforce is creating a need to develop new sources of talent. The propagation and access to knowledge on the internet have given increase to the greater demand for the ability to distinguish fact from opinion. These trends, among others, are changing the way people learn and making investments in employee training and development more critical in shaping the success of an organization than it has been in the past. (Tarique, 2014) Millennial leaders have helped companies to build a better workplace and most of the team building has been centered around building a stronger organization overall that is unified. Not every person that walks into work is going to be excited about someone younger than their age group leading as a manager. Millennials have worked hard to earn their place in leadership and in management. According to Longenecker, **"**Managers recognized a series of problems caused by ineffective management training problems not produced by millennials. An overview of these findings were created to define how organizations have been inadequate in training. Findings suggest that the efficiency of management training has a significant impact on managerial and managerial performance." (Longenecker, 2005)

Gone are the days that you enter into a face and your manager if half your age. With modern management the managers may be younger than or even the same age as their employees. Age does not convey someone's ability to lead or not to lead however it is experience, education and skills that help to set the millennial manager apart from other leaders in the company. Millennials have now been trained to be leading examples in the company and to work towards leading and one day owning the companies that they manage. As a manager the millennial has a responsibility to both their organization and to their teams that they are leading to stand out and to lead in excellence. Age should not be the definitive to why someone is a leader in a company but it their experience and leadership ability that helps them to stand out and to lead effectively.

Psychological Needs in Management

There are times in management to which the needs have not been properly met for leaders to lead effectively. What is meant by this is that managers have not properly mentally prepared themselves for the responsibility that has been incurred. A great example of the human law of needs is in Maslow's Hierarchy of needs which reflects on how if the needs are met it helps to make a difference in leadership. Abraham Maslow approached the study of personality by focusing on subjective experiences, free will, and the innate drive toward self-actualization. Maslow expanded the field of humanistic psychology to include an explanation of how human needs change throughout an individual's lifespan, and how these needs influence the development of personality. Maslow's hierarchy of needs ranks human needs from the most basic physical needs to the most advanced needs of self-actualization. A person must acquire and dominate each level of need before proceeding to the next need." (http://www.boundless.com, 2016) The same is

14

such in management for millennials. They learn and share through experience, socialization, and respect. With age comes a level of maturity but for some there is often the emotional turbulence that comes in the way that interferes with daily emotions. Millennial managers have learned how to not allow their emotions to get the best of them in the workplace and how to be temperamental when needed. In today's society where getting noticed at times takes drastic measures, leaders have to sometimes deal with the psychological outcomes that are incurred through to premature leadership. An understanding of basic humanistic needs helps a millennial manager to understand the needs of employees that they are leading. The ability to understand and then articulate the needs of others in an organization helps to build lasting companies. The rate of retention is them expanded in an organization to which employees feel appreciated and valued. A millennial that understands the emotional and psychological needs of others is one that is to be praised. In companies that understand the sentiment and value of those within their organizations it builds a family of support and understanding. Millennial managers are rising to the challenge of leadership and gaining the psychological acumen to withstand and endure the challenges that are accompanied with leading others.

Mentoring New Millennials into Management

In the presence of greatness there is always someone who is greater to help unleash true potential. That potential is revealed through mentorship. Millennials benefit from having a mentor in management because it helps to create value in leadership as well as student mentality. Mentorship propels leaders to aim higher in leadership. It is important for millennials to learn how to seize the moment in leadership and truly embrace it. Leadership is not always easy but it is rewarding to have a mentor to trust and confide in and to share decisions with when needed. A mentor is there to support and assist the millennial manager with their new role. There are some managers that are natural born leaders that will require little or minimal mentoring time. The important factor for the millennial manager is to learn how to embrace what is given through mentorship and to never stop learning. There is so much to give through the influence that is shared and partnered in mentorship. There will be ups and downs but in the end the mentor will help to push the mentee to their fullest potential. One of the advantages that I have seen young adults in management is that they have an opportunity to reach out to numerous connections and numerous mentors. However, it is the one mentor that stands beside your decisions and supports your leadership that truly helps the millennial manager to blossom into the true leader that they are in the workplace. Some people do not do well under pressure or as a leader they have the right skills and knowledge to lead but lack the emotional candor that is needed to exercise the position of a manager. A mentor helps a millennial manager to grow and to develop into their full potential as a manager and leader.

Fulfilling Needs in Management

The best trait than millennials can share as a promise of security to others is the ability of others to trust or gain trust from their leadership. In order for the leader to be followed they must prove to others around them that they are in fact trustworthy. The needs of the company are to fill managerial roles with leaders that can be trusted. As Paul McDonald, senior executive director of the specialized staffing firm Robert Half International, puts it, the oldest millennials are entering management roles as baby boomers enter the "sunset of their careers." (McMullen, 2014) Managers have to adapt to the needs of others in the workplace. It is often easy for the manager to see the need of their own learning style versus the needs of others. Leaders are often apt to develop an inclination to the training that has been initiated. However, the basic skills in training are not always fulfilled due to the learning styles, training curriculums, training programs, and leadership development program structures. Sebrell asserted that the training management system should be knowledgeable of handling registrations for all levels of study and training. It should have the forecasting capability as well. Only a few training management software packages are currently available commercially. The mandate for well-designed training management system products will grow as corporations move to strategic systems and realize that the magnitude and value of technical training can contribute to their competitive advantage and drive for better production in training. (Sebrell, 1989)

Training and management are two components in business that are essential to the development and growth of the millennial leader. There are management training programs often referred to as management in training programs that offer managers the opportunity to learn how to be an effective manager and train to be an effective manager for a company. The management training program offers a potential manager an opportunity to develop leadership skills while working to become a lead manager in the company.

Managers in training are often given minimal tasks that are to be carried out in the workplace or often placed in vigorous programs that require a time commitment of six months to a year to fulfill the management training requirements. Management training programs that are more personally driven through employee focus are more promising for future leaders to look up to when to determine which type of management training works the best. In a recent article by Thomas Walsh, it stated that Often times it is the famous coaches that in turn capture the teams that are endearing. However, it is teams that are created by not always including those who are the best to be a part of the team. If all the team is constructed of winners, then the team will become one that will end up underperforming. If teams are framed to win in the beginning it will then create a team that always wins in the long run in training. (Walsh, 2013)

Dale Carnegie's Training Program

Training helps to keep companies innovative and fresh with the latest tools and technology to continue in business. According to Solnik, a lot of companies has developed a great appreciation for those in leadership that have mastered the art of both leadership and training. Companies now have paid to send their managers to a training program that has been designed by the leadership constructs of Dale Carnegie. Leadership and management courses are popular at global companies in China, while leadership skills for young people are popular in Taiwan. More companies have now decided to use this training program because of the results that have been demonstrated through the training. (Solnik, 2012)

The new incoming millennial leaders now have an opportunity to participate in Dale Carnegie training programs. According to Bawaba, creating better training programs that are youth centered are important for the Dale

Carnegie Training program. Training for young adults has been offered through Dale Carnegie Training specifically in the United States and has met with overwhelming success. The Dale Carnegie Team is enthusiastic about this new valued partnership with Michigan State University Dubai, which has shown 100 per cent commitment to the education of young adults, ensuring they are confident and well equipped to face the challenges of today's business world, added Rasha Zeitoun. There is great promise and aspirations that have been derived that are full of expectancies which are for today's young adults with their entire soft skill requirements, developing them into tomorrow's future leaders. (Sawaba, 2010)

Why the Millennial Generation?

The millennial generation has been acknowledged and recognized as the next leaders of the future. Millennial leaders are most driven and inspired by technology and independence. They have a keen awareness of computers, technology, and digital access. More millennials now are becoming self-made millionaires and have opted to pursue their own careers and open their own businesses as entrepreneurs.

According to Murray, many generations have emerged in response to the technology that has been created for leaders all over the world. A great number of millennials take on leadership positions within academic libraries, their attitudes towards and uses of technology may bring conflicting expectations for leadership to the forefront. What has proven to cause major captivations of millennial leaders? What are some areas of areas of concerns that have created stress on millennials. (Murray, 2011) Meister and Willyerd assert that millennials, the makeup of the global workforce are undergoing an economical shifting. In about four years, millennials which were born between 1977 and 1997 will represent half the employees in the world. In some companies, they already constitute a majority. That shift may sound daunting to the managers charged with coaching these young workers, who have a reputation for being attention sponges. However, our research into the varying expectations and needs of employees across four generations has given us a more nuanced view of Millennials and uncovered several resource efficient ways to mentor them. (Meister & Willyerd, 2010)

According to Gentry, Managers from different generations have considered certain leadership practices important for how the success is carried out within an organization, whether managers were skilled in those leadership practices, there was, however, a gap between the perceived importance and the skill ratings. (Gentry, 2011) Chou asserts millennial leaders as, the millennial Generation in the workplace has received major responsiveness as it has been shown that millennials equate different attitudes, values, beliefs, and aspirations in the workplace compared to the previous generations. Although numerous studies have devoted to the exploration of millennials, the leadership and followership styles exhibited by millennials at work has been largely neglected. The major purpose of this article is to develop a conceptual framework that explores millennials' leadership and followership styles in the workplace. By exploring and observing millennials in the context of leadership and followership, this article provides important theoretical and practical implications. (Chou, 2012)

Andert asserts millennial leadership as, the current four-generational workforce becomes a more youthful three-generational workforce, holding a controlled collaboration, hierarchal focus as dominate will most likely lead to organizational strife. Organizations need inclusive, innovative and dynamic workplace opportunities. Successful models of interactive organizations, expanding worker synergies are present in such new-generational firms as Zappos, Google, Amazon, and Facebook. (Andert, 2011)

Balda and Mora asserted that current research offers a complex perspective on the main characteristics of millennials as a generation in which knowledge is acquired, shared, and created as an extension of the primacy of

25

relationships and networks and embedded in the connections that information technology provides. Millennial were most recognized among leaders that were servant leaders. However, theories developed in previous generations are not automatically applicable and require critical examination and adaptation if they are to offer an understanding of means for motivating and influencing Millennials toward more broadly defined goals and aspirations in multigenerational workplaces.

The Leadership Ability of Millennials

In leadership, it is imperative to have a leader in place that is both knowledgeable and skilled in the area in which they have been positioned to lead. Leaders that were born between 1980 through 2000 have been labeled as Millennial Leaders. Leaders that have evolved from this time period and era have often resorted to leading through entrepreneurship and utilizing their expertise and knowledge in their own businesses and companies. Millennial leadership has helped to change leadership through creativity and leadership thinking that is more out of the box. Millennial leadership has infiltrated now as the new face of leadership. It comes as no surprise that different generations respond to and utilize emerging technology in to their advantage. More millennials take on leadership positions within more challenging workplaces, their attitudes towards and uses of technology may bring conflicting expectations for leadership to the forefront. What are the generational traits and motivations of the Millennial and how will they manifest themselves as a style of leadership? (Murray, 2011) The article discusses the provision of leadership development to employees from the millennial generation, focusing on the results of the "Leadership Development for Millennials: Why It Matters" study from the American Society for Training and Development and the Institute for Corporate Productivity. According to the article, Millennials are attracted to organizations that offer learning and development opportunities, but many Millennials do not possess leadership or social skills. Topics include on-the-job training, tuition reimbursement for continuing education, and transferable career skills. (Lykins & Pace, 2013)

The Millennial Trainer/Manager

Millennial leaders have the passion, resilience, and tenacity that it takes to become long lasting leaders that lead effectively. Millennials are driven by success and will hard to gain money to secure a foundation for their families as well as gain wealth and stability. There may be times when the millennial has to manage others in various age groups. McCullen asserted that, whenever you're managing someone who is older than you, you want to know your stuff, but you don't want to be a know-it-all," says Courtney Templin, chief operating officer of JB Training Solutions and co-author of "Manager 3.0: A Millennial's Guide to Rewriting the Rules of Management." "Know when to listen and when to recognize,

'Maybe I don't know everything about this situation. (McCullen, 2014) It is important for millennial managers to bring their A game to the workplace and to show that they have the lasting presence in leading that is used to make an impact. The millennial manager at times can play the role of the training manager because they have to teach and train others in the company on the company's needs and goals. As a millennial trainer or manager millennials help to bring in creativity and agility to the workplace that helps to build an environment of innovation and substance.

Why Millennials are highly sought out leaders

Born between 1980 and 2000, raised by Baby Boomer parents to seek out and find information, question the status quo, and embrace their potential to make a difference. Millennials or Gen Y brings their generational mindset to their work as managers. Despite the exuberance and energy that millennials have they are highly subject to being stereotyped (http://www.proquest.com, 2015) Leaders such as Barbara Rapaport has decided to build a consulting and branding business that specializes in helping millennial leaders to succeed. The consulting business includes a four-week intensive class that is geared for millennials. According to Weick, Barbara Rapaport, founder, and president of Real-Time Perspectives Inc. is launching new programs have been designed exclusively for millennials to participate and gain leadership training. (Weick, 2015) With leadership sessions as such, this creates promise for millennials that are looking to enhance their career and to have development.

Millennials are saying we are hiring

The most refreshing word to hear or email to receive after being interviewed are the words *you are hired.* Millennials now are the interviewers in the room that are looking hire people of all backgrounds. Millennials stand proud to say the words now hiring to others from their companies and post bulletins on social media for advertising to celebrate the company and the future employees that are being hired. They have now formulated their own brand in terms of identity and classification. Millennials are force to be reckoned with. They may seem like the pushover leader but they are anything far from being a pushover and they have the character, leadership, and strength to prove their abilities. Now when millennials say the words you are hired it means more to new employees it's an opportunity to gain employment from someone that is often in a peer age group or close and it makes coming to work a more enjoyable moment to look forward to. I had one of the best millennial managers when I worked at a company called West in Tulsa Oklahoma. She was 25 years old and she was in college working on her degree in business and she was very driven. I admired her style of leadership it was based on celebrating her team whenever possible she would decorate their desks and place a balloon on the back of the chairs and give them candy. I gave her the nickname of Boss Lady because even though she was young she knew how to carry herself at all times and she knew when to be professional and when to be herself. She represented millennial women that are courageous and inspiring that are mothers, students, leaders, and the future CEO's of the company. Another great millennial leader that I had in the same company was also in his 20's and he was very detail oriented and fun to have as a manager. Millennials know how to manage other millennials and they also know how to manage others that are not in their age brackets as well. Millennials bring that to the table in management their creativity, fun, support, encouragement, and innovation.

Millennials and Technology

Global companies that are looking to hire leaders that have both technology skills and training will definitely find the skills that they are seeking through a millennial leader. Giantasio included that, "In response to the numbers obtained over the years it is evident that millennials ages 18-34 are a major cultural factor not just in the advertising business but the country overall. The U.S. has roughly 75 million millennials, and this year they are projected to become the single largest segment of the American workforce. In the advertising industry, millennials now make up 44 percent of the workforce which is an 8 percent rise since 2010. It is now become like before the march of the millennials. (Giantasio, 2016) The Randstad Technology reveals that millennials are the ones to reach out for upcoming Information Technology leadership positions. In a recent article by Randstad Technologies it stated that millennials have grown up in a digital society with technology touching almost every aspect of their lives, said Bob Dickey, Group President of Technology and Engineering, Randstad Technologies. As a result, millennials want to have the same technological capabilities in the workplace as they have in their personal lives. To attract and retain millennial talent, IT leaders need to rapidly adopt current and forward-thinking technologies into their infrastructures. Organizations that are unable to support millennials' IT needs may see greater turnover and experience more difficulty recruiting top talent from this demographic of the workforce. (

https://www.randstadusa.com/workforce360/workforce,

2015) More colleges today are graduating students that have

degrees in both IT and in business. The growing number has

now prepared an opportunity for millennials to start their own

company or they can come in as entry level employees and

start their career path as a future manager. Based on the skill

and the expertise of the employee it then will enhance

promotion for the millennial based off of the hiring

manager's approval.

Millennials are Ambitious and Tenacious

Millennials are the aspiring face of leadership both in

the workplace and as entrepreneurs. As leaders, they have the

maturity, ambition, and tenacity that is needed to manage a

company of their own as well for an organization. In a recent

study conducted by Dill she included that, "It's extremely

important that employers pay attention to the Millennial

generation," said Lars Zander, Universum global CMO,

"since in only 10 years they will make up 75% of the

workforce, compared to only 25% today. Forty-one percent of respondents said taking on a leadership or management role was "very" important to them. The greatest percentage of respondents, 35, said this was because of compensation, but almost as many, 31%, said their motivation was a desire for authority and leadership." (Dill, 2015) Millennials are not afraid to apply for management positions or to seek out opportunities for leadership. Their energy helps them to leap over all obstacles and to go after their dreams. Millennial leaders have an adrenaline that forces them to want more in life and not to settle for less. They will try new things, try out careers, try out jobs, and try out managerial positions because at times they may become bored and want to try something new and fresh. They are courageous and brave and have the inertia that allows them the ability to master more than one skill and level in leadership positions. They have the ability to walk and chew gum at the same time in management because they are good at multi-tasking and they are risk takers.

The Millennial Difference

Ng, Schweitzer, and Lyons wrote a very interesting article on the effects of millennial leaders of a job. They had realistic expectations of their first job and salary but were seeking rapid advancement and the development of new skills, while also ensuring a meaningful and satisfying life outside of work. Our results suggest that Millennials' expectations and values vary by gender, visible minority status, GPA, and year of study, but these variables explain only a small proportion of variance. Changing North American demographics have created a crisis in organizations as they strive to recruit and retain the millennial generation, who purportedly hold values, attitudes, and expectations that are significantly different from those of the generations of workers that preceded them. A better understanding of the Millennials' career expectations and priorities helps employers to create job offerings and work environments that are more likely to engage and retain millennial workers. (Ng, Schweitzer, & Lyons, 2010)

Leaders have a certain aurora about them that sets them apart from others which is the same for millennial leaders they have a strong leadership style that sets them apart from others. Millennials are not satisfied with the old way of doing things and they invite change and use change within their workplaces very often because it helps to create a culture that is accustomed to change management and one that has an appreciation for the changes that are to come within the workplace.

Millennials are Innovative and Talented

Millennials are very educated and some start fresh out of college into their careers as entrepreneurs. In places of employment that are not as, diverse millennials work hard to find acceptance through their degrees, certifications, and internships. According to Yuki, from January to October 2015, U.S. brands published 35 million posts across

Facebook, Twitter, and Instagram, sparking 65 billion actions with social audiences. Yet just 7 percent of these actions involved sharing of a brand's content. Despite what is increasingly recognized as the value of shared content for building brand equity, to the author's knowledge, there has been a scant study on what actually makes content shareable and the psychological drivers that prompt sharing. Replicating an earlier framework that outlined ways to increase the vitality of content, the author tracked the 2,000 most-shared social posts over a 12-month period on Facebook and then surveyed more than 10,000 social media users about what might drive them to share that content online. (Yuki, 2015) Both Millennial men and women rank high in terms of leadership. A recent study acknowledged how women millennial leaders were successful. It stated, "It is concluded that the expansion of identity alternatives creates both opportunities and challenges for professional Millennial women that have implications for consumer wellbeing and service providers. Directions for future research and insights for marketers, particularly service providers, are discussed and it remains unclear how the growing influence and buying the power of this new generation of women will impact the marketplace. This uncertainty is compounded by the lack of cultural agreement regarding roles and responsibilities of an educated professional woman regarding work, family, and personal development. (Ball, 2014)

Millennials have learned from generations prior to them about the value of having goals and putting them into practice early on in life. In an article about valuing time, Hobart and Sendeck asserted that "Many leaders have gone unrecognized for their commitment and dedication to an organization. In prior years working at a company until retirement was the only way that was recognized to gain pensions and social security. Fast forward many years the generation has now changed it is now one that is full of aspiring leaders, entrepreneurs and millennials that have taken a new turn in how living till retirement is effectively accomplished. Generations that were once dedicated and loyal to work are now loyal to their positions such as training. In the past employees stayed at companies for long periods of time in hopes of gaining something in return. Now times have changed and the workplace is now a training setting for some to gain new experience and learn the skills needed to obtain employment for the next job or career path that had been intended. The days of loyalty have expired but have now been replaced with millennials in management. They represent a replica of leaders of the future compared to the leaders of the past generations that were loyal and stayed more than thirty years at an organization. There are a lot of hard-working young adult managers that have a loyalty to hard work and proper training produce results for employees as well as higher retention rates for the company. (Hobart & Sendek, 2014) According to Khan, proper training is defined as, training has the distinct role in the achievement of an organizational goal by incorporating the interests of the organization and the workforce. (Khan, 2011)

40

Millennials are Well Recognized by Employers

The highly opinionated Millennial brings a unique goal-oriented work style to his or her work environment. Zemke, Raines, and Filipczak (2000) revealed in studies that 80% of Millennials surveyed "believe that hard work and goal setting are the keys to achieving their dreams" and "had already established specific goals for the next five years" (p. 144). Millennials desire variety in the workplace, and their work ethic reflects this. Millennials are critical of the typical normal workday and environment; they prefer more freedom in terms of job schedules and flexible lifestyles. They also want the best technology to create a highly collaborative

41

environment those folds easily into a healthy work/life balance (Tapscott, 2009, p. 300)

For things lie career goals, employee engagement, preferred leadership styles and recognition, Millennial share many of the same attitudes as Gen X and Baby Boomer employees, an IBM study revealed. In the multigenerational study which covered some 1,800 employees from organizations of all sizes, across 12 countries, IBM found that the basic distinction between Millennials and older employees is their digital competence, which comes from growing up immersed in a digital world. Within the next five years, Millennials are expected to wield increasing influence over organizations' decisions, move into leadership roles and basically take over the workforce." (http://www.ProQuest.com, 2015) Millennial leaders are the pulse of the workplace. A workplace that has millennials will have diversity and creativity. Farrell and Hurt assert millennial leadership in the workplace as the millennial generation enters the workforce it is becoming increasingly essential that members of the workforce understand this generation. Understanding how the millennial generation learns can assist trainers and instructional designers in creating effective training programs. (Farrell & Hurt, 2014)

Millennials going Global

Global leadership training creates cultural awareness and sensitivity for the potential manager to have a better understanding of the country and its business standards. Global leadership training should offer the managers an opportunity to build relationship and report while at the same time maintaining ethical standards. Global leadership training provides the learner an opportunity to manage employees in a different country. One great attribute to a technologically driven society is the added benefit of providing training rooms with the best computers and in this, it helps with creating the best environments for training. An enhanced learning environment helps to promote awareness and increase knowledge through creativity and innovation. Global leadership training is required for leaders that are upcoming in the marketplace. A training environment that has the latest technology helps to provide a more in-depth training atmosphere that is thought to provoke and helps increase the learner's creativity while in the training setting. Millennials learn through touch screens, smartphones, tablets, ebooks, and electronics.

According to Tarique, the trends that capture workplace training and development are changing in so many ways the knowledge economy is growing and becoming an inevitable part of the modern business structure. Jobs are becoming more fluid and specialized. The aging of the workforce is creating a need to develop new sources of talent. The proliferation and access to knowledge on the Internet have given rise to the greater demand for the ability to discern fact from opinion. These trends, among others, are changing the way people learn and making investments in employee training and development more critical in determining the success of an organization than it has been in the past. (Tarique, 2014)

The millennial leadership styles have been challenged due to the level of competition in the workplace between other leaders that are within the same age range and leaders that are older in age. There are however future aspirations for the millennial leader to introduce a new level of leadership and training to the global marketplace one that has been long overdue for the global market. Global leaders exude a level of leadership that is most influential in that the leadership involves a lot more interaction from a virtual leadership setting, more trust is expected, and leaders that are representing their countries in a different country have to also have a strong level of communication which helps to build a better leadership and global business.

Holt and Kyoko also described how the global leader in the future will make an impact on the world. They asserted that, in The 2020 Workplace, Jeanne Meister and Karie Willyerd describe additional forces that are shaping the workplace-including mobile technology and social learning. People around the world are now bound together by our interconnectedness as well as economic uncertainty. People everywhere are asking what it takes to be an effective global leader. With all the shifts happening in the world and in our workforce, we need new types of global leaders to help organizations navigate complexity and change. (Holt & Kyoko, 2012)

The key to keeping the attention of a millennial leader in training is to provide resources that are interesting, fun and catch their attention the moment the millennials enter a training classroom. Some training environments of managers have been known to be very vigorous for managers in training. The new launch of leadership has helped to provide a better consensus of leadership through proper According to Tarique, the impact of technology on learning and workplace training and development can be traced back to 1970 with the emergence of computer-assisted learning using mainframe computers. The early 2000s were a replica of learning opportunities that optimizes training programs. (Tarique, 2014)

Creating Global Leadership Training Awareness

In business it is often easier to help take the load off of other leaders that have been hired as managers. Through offering a compensation package that includes relocation fees for moving costs and reimbursement for fees, it is not always easy for leaders to transition to other countries well without the proper support, guidance, and cultural awareness that is needed to endure living in another country. According to Brookwood Relocation services it asserted that moving to a foreign location can be a stressful process," said Scott Sullivan, executive vice president, Brookfield Global Relocation Services. Over the last 50 years, the Intercultural Group has pioneered the right combination of assessment, training, and coaching to maximize the success for globally mobile employees and their families. Our proprietary

intercultural training prepares a transferring employee and

their family by providing them with the awareness,

knowledge, and skills needed to adapt to living and working

in a new location. This support also benefits employers by

helping to ensure a successful transition for the entire family

to avoid potentially time-consuming and costly mistakes of a

failed assignment. (Brookwood B.G., 2013) According to

Reed, According to the consulting firm Workplace

Trends, 83% of employees have worked with a millennial

manager at some point, while outlets such

as *Parade* report that a full quarter of the generation

has reached leadership roles in their companies. Globally a

whopping 62% of under-35s are in positions where they

supervise the work of others.

Global Leadership Takes a New Role in Defining Leadership for Millennials

Leadership has taken a newly defined role in the incorporation of how leadership is viewed through a global stance. Global leadership is a more intense platform in leadership than most due to the cultural barrios that often occur due to the challenges that are faced as a global leader. According to Safty, today the information and communication revolution has changed its view of sovereignty and made its relevance tenuous. Globalization has defeated protectionism. Economic liberalism has diminished the power and size of many states. Although the challenges facing the world are formidable, our leaders are no longer larger than life. In fact, political leadership is in many places in a state of crisis. Despite this, many in the media still equate leaders with political leadership. (Safty, 1999) McDougall and David asserted that a global leader must also demonstrate a strong leadership aptitude as well as a global mindset. In terms of emotional intelligence, the globally minded leader has to possess the ability to manage both their actions, and the actions of others as well provide empathy for those around their circle of influence. (McDougall &McDavid, 2014)

Companies today are gravitating more to millennial leaders because of the insight, innovation, and creativity that they offer. In 2016 leadership for millennials will become one that is welcoming new millennial leaders. In a recent article from a press conference review it stated that cities now were going to entrust millennials as mayors. In 2016, for the first time, more millennials will be eligible to vote than baby boomers. A new national political group, Action for America, will announce a major new initiative aimed at recruiting millennials to run for public office. Laquan D. Austin, the CEO of Action for America, will be then announcing the group's new initiative to get more millennial candidates into the electoral process. Action for America, an affiliate of Run for America, is geared towards working with millennial candidates across the country in this year's elections. (http://www.prnewsletter.com, 2016). The inspiration of having a millennial as a future mayor is also an expectation for business leaders to have millennials not only as the training managers of the future but as the CEO's of major global organizations in the future. Millennials have helped to change the viewpoint of leadership through their technological skillsets, education, and experience.

Global Millennial Leader in Management

According to newswire.com, it is evident now more than ever that the business world of the mid-21st century, driven by the soon-to-be-dominant millennial generation, will be very different from that of the past. According to a recent study by Bentley University, millennials, who will make up 75% of the American workforce by 2025, have developed their own unique vision of success. In the study, only a very small minority 13% of surveyed millennials young professionals born in and after the early to mid-1980s—said that their career goal involved climbing the corporate ladder to become a CEO or president. In contrast, nearly two-thirds 66% said that their career goal involves starting and running their own business. (http://www.newswire.com, 2014)

Millennials leading in global leadership as managers will help to create diversity in leadership all over the world. Millennials are helping to bridge the gaps in leadership. Millennials are working as the next generation of future leaders. Millennials aspire to be the next leaders that can help to bring innovation and change to training programs. "Millennials believe business has a responsibility to help solve the world's problems, but they don't expect them to do it alone. Fifty-one percent of those surveyed said they want to personally get involved in making the world a better place. Millennials are vocal to their opinions of what they desire therefore companies are adapting to the styles of millennial leadership. Sixty-nine percent want companies and employers to make it easier for them to do their part, such as donating a portion of product proceeds to causes they care about, giving them time off to volunteer and providing activities they can participate in. (http://www.newswire.com, 2014)

Millennial Managers Are Making a Difference

Throughout the world millennial managers are working hard to create atmospheres within the workplace that are most conducive for their employees. Millennial managers help to make a difference through their constant care and attention to their workplaces and employees as well as to their dedication to other managers. The most powerful way to make a difference is to realize that there is room to make a difference. Millennial managers have adapted to the customs and traditions of management but they have also helped to contribute a share of their own styles into leadership. Workplaces that used to have conservative dress codes and no tattoos are more lenient towards the dress code now and more adept to the person that is wearing the clothes' personality, gifts, and contributions to the workplace. Millennial managers may look different from other managers and have certain quirks about them in leadership but that is what sets them apart from other leaders. Millennial managers are stepping away from their once known comfort zones and into the lime light of leadership. There are great expectations in store for the millennial leader and there is so much that they can contribute to their workplaces. The workplaces that hire millennials as managers now are no longer taking a risk but they are helping to improve the workplace by having a millennial leader that is responsible and in charge. Millennial leaders are not just leaders in fast food workplaces such as McDonalds but they are also major leaders in corporate America.

Why is Millennial Management Different?

According to a recent article by Reed, for years, Millennials have been the staple youth of the workforce, recent college grads and junior employees just starting to work their way up the ladder. Lately things have changed. Millennials have gotten more common at the office, overtaking Generation X as the largest generation in the workforce, and they've gotten older. Many are now in their mid-30s, buying houses and starting families." (Reed,

2016) Millennials are even retiring earlier than most because they have started their own companies as an entrepreneur and it has prospered or they have learned how to successful invest well in stock to save for their future. The internet provides so many resources that are available to young adults more than ever before in history. In age where you can order a robot online, Google directions, video chat over the phone, and text appointments it has now come to be known as the age of socialization for our world. Millennials function differently because they have the technical resources to help them to do so in leadership. Long are the days of writing lists when it can be instant messaged or sent as a voice note on the phone. Millennial managers are more technologically driven than most because they have the tools to lead effectively. Millennials enjoy being challenged while at work. According to stats from a 2011 survey, almost half of hiring managers believe "high pay" is most important to millennials, compared to only 27% of actual millennials. Meanwhile, managers significantly underestimate how much millennials prioritize "meaningful work" and the importance they place on feeling a "sense of accomplishment."(Meeker, 2011) Millennials work hard and they should be compensated well for their hard work and commitment to their workplaces.

How to embrace the management shift

The best way to embrace the management shift is to appreciate it more through helping to celebrate the millennials that you see in leadership and help to keep them motivated as leaders. The management shift that is present is not easy for everyone to embrace and for some it is hard to have someone leading that is younger than the anticipated age group. Maturity and skill is what it all measures down to be in leadership. Change in commands is important even in leadership. Generational changes through employers helps to carry the torch for the next leaders that are to come.

Standing out in leadership as a millennial

If you are a current millennial manager I would like to congratulate you on reaching that level of leadership. It comes with hard work and dedication and you have definitely proven the skills, education, and leadership that are needed to lead as a young adult. All over the workplaces all over the world, millennials are the true face of modern leadership. In offices you will find young budding leaders providing feedback to their teams, coaching, leading, inspiring, and managing their teams to the best of their ability. There will be loud cheers of celebration across the workplaces, excitement, and anticipation for what the new modern leader has to bring to the table in leadership and in management. The millennial leader is the new face of leadership worldwide and the trending decadence of newfound joy is now being embraced in workplaces throughout the nation. It is not just important to be a leader that is a young adult but to be a leader that is replica of generations that are to come. It is important to stand out as a millennial leader and to not allow anyone, anything, or any circumstance to stand in the way of the leadership that is locked inside. It is important to go above and beyond in leadership and make a mark that everyone remembers. No one remembers a leader who has not done anything to be remembered for in life but everyone will remember a leader that has demonstrated sacrifice, character, loyalty, morality, communication, resilience, and innovative creations. They will also remember a leader that cares, stays up to check on their team, is there when an employee is in the hospital, is there when an employee wins a competition, is there to comfort when an employee loses a loved one, is there when someone from the team passes away, and they are also remembered for always going the extra mile in the workplace for their teams. The way for millennial leaders to stand out is to not be average and to practice not being mediocre and always keeping creativity active in the workplace to keep the company refreshed and alive.

Staying connected with a strong leadership network

It is important to build a leader network and to stay connected with other managers and leaders. Leaders should always remember that they are never alone as managers. They should know that there is always someone there to provide mentorship and support. Through building a strong leadership network it helps to formulate accountability, discipline, trust, and networking skills. The purpose of the strong network is to help the millennial leader to grow and develop effectively. A strong team helps them to have a shoulder to cry on when needed, a support for encouragement, and a sounding board for ideas and future strategies. Not every network will be the same each will be diverse in its own right and provide the guidance that is needed for future millennial leaders. The network can also provide social media support through having a Facebook accountability team, building connections on Linkedin, and workplace group teams. Accountability goes a long way in leadership and millennials that build strong leadership network connections are going to see proven results for their teams and for their future teams.

When a millennial manager introduces themselves with the words, *Hello my name is* it will now resonate a better sound to the world that the millennial can be proud of infiltrating and that is the sound of knowing that their name means more than just an average employee their name means manager, future CEO, world leader, future entrepreneur, but most importantly that their name means that they are one that has been hired to provide the necessary training, development, and growth that is needed the most for the employees and the team. The next time you see are hired to a new position and work and it is a millennial that is your manager remember that they are the new modern faces of leadership and that they have been well equipped and trained to lead your team and that this will be one of the best years of your life because you have a millennial leader that is going to motivate and inspire you to your fullest potential.

About the Author

Monique L. Rodgers was born and reared in Newark, NJ. She is a millennial and she understands the mindset of a millennial leader. She is first generation college student that obtained her Bachelor's degree from Oral Roberts University in Tulsa, Oklahoma. She obtained her Masters of Science in Management degree from Colorado Technical University and she will be graduating in March 2017 with a Doctorate of Management degree from Colorado Technical University.

She's a member of Victorious Praise Fellowship COGIC in Durham NC where she serves as an usher. She is an international speaker and leader. She's a member of Toastmasters International where she has won speech contests and achieved Competent Leader and Communicator in 2014, She is a recent member of International Distinguished Scholars, Who's Who amongst Business Leaders and Professionals 2010-2011, and CLEO's Scholars. She enjoys writing, singing, researching, traveling, and reading. She has traveled to five countries. She aspires to help mentor young adults and encourage millennials to continue to lead and make a difference in the world through management.

www.ingramcontent.com/pod-product-compliance
Lightning Source LLC
Chambersburg PA
CBHW040846180526
45159CB00001B/330